Trees

Level 5 – Green

Helpful Hints for Reading at Home

The graphemes (written letters) and phonemes (units of sound) used throughout this series are aligned with Letters and Sounds. This offers a consistent approach to learning, weather reading at home or in the classroom.

HERE IS A LIST OF NEW PHONEMES FOR THIS PHASE OF LEARNING. AN EXAMPLE OF THE PRONUNCIATION CAN BE FOUND IN BRACKETS.

Phase 5			
ay (day)	ou (out)	ie (tie)	ea (eat)
oy (boy)	ir (girl)	ue (blue)	aw (saw)
wh (when)	ph (photo)	ew (new)	oe (toe)
au (Paul)	a_e (make)	e_e (these)	i_e (like)
o_e (home)	u_e (rule)		

Phase 5 Alternative Pronunciations of Graphemes			
a (hat, what)	e (bed, she)	i (fin, find)	o (hot, so, other)
u (but, unit)	c (cat, cent)	g (got, giant)	ow (cow, blow)
ie (tied, field)	ea (eat, bread)	er (farmer, herb)	ch (chin, school, chef)
y (yes, by, very)	ou (out, shoulder, could, you)		

HERE ARE SOME WORDS WHICH YOUR CHILD MAY FIND TRICKY.

Phase 5 Tricky Words			
oh	their	people	Mr
Mrs	looked	called	asked
could			

TOP TIPS FOR HELPING YOUR CHILD TO READ:

- Allow children time to break down unfamiliar words into units of sound and then encourage children to string these sounds together to create the word.

- Encourage your child to point out any focus phonics when they are used.

- Read through the book more than once to grow confidence.

- Ask simple questions about the text to assess understanding.

- Encourage children to use illustrations as prompts.

This book focuses on the phoneme /ir/ and is a Green level 5 book band.

How many words can you list with ir in?

Answers: bird, first, third, thirsty, dirt.

Trees start out as seeds. When a seed has all that it needs, a root will press into the dirt.

A shoot will then spring up from the top. It will soon be a seedling, then a sapling.

Seedling

Sapling

A tree will have a slim trunk in its first year. Some trees might need support in strong wind.

Trunk

This tree is in its third year. Its trunk is thicker and can support lemons.

When a tree is big, it has a firm trunk and branches. Its roots go deep into the dirt.

Tree roots can extend out a long way.
They need wet dirt to absorb water from.

Roots

A tree's girth is how thick or thin it is. A big tree needs lots of people to get their arms around it.

You can see how long a tree has been there by checking the number of rings it has.

Rings

Some trees are dormant in winter, such as birch trees. They will bud again in the summer.

Birch trees

Some trees are green all year, such as fir trees. The snow will not kill them.

Fir trees

If you see a mess of twigs high up on a branch, that might not be part of the tree.

That mess of twigs might be a nest that a bird has set up to keep its eggs in!

©2023 **BookLife Publishing Ltd.**
King's Lynn, Norfolk, PE30 4LS, UK.

ISBN 978-1-80505-062-9

All rights reserved. Printed in China.
A catalogue record for this book is available from the British Library.

Trees
Written by Charis Mather
Designed by Barry Onions

MIX
Paper from responsible sources
FSC® C113515

An Introduction to BookLife Readers...

Our Readers have been specifically created in line with the London Institute of Education's approach to book banding and are phonetically decodable and ordered to support each phase of the Letters and Sounds document.

Each book has been created to provide the best possible reading and learning experience. Our aim is to share our love of books with children, providing both emerging readers and prolific page-turners with beautiful books that are guaranteed to provoke interest and learning, regardless of ability.

BOOK BAND GRADED using the Institute of Education's approach to levelling.

PHONETICALLY DECODABLE supporting each phase of Letters and Sounds.

EXERCISES AND QUESTIONS to offer reinforcement and to ascertain comprehension.

CLEAR DESIGN to inspire and provoke engagement, providing the reader with clear visual representations of each non-fiction topic.

AUTHOR INSIGHT:
CHARIS MATHER

Charis Mather is a children's author at BookLife Publishing who has a love for reading and writing. Her studies in linguistics and experiences working with young readers have given her a knack for writing material that suits a range of ages and skill levels. Charis is passionate about producing books that emphasise the fun in reading and is convinced that no matter how much you already know, there is always something new to learn.

This book focuses on /ir/ and is a Green level 5 book band.

Image Credits Images are courtesy of Shutterstock.com. With thanks to Getty Images, Thinkstock Photo and iStockphoto. Cover – WARUT PINAMKA, AlyonaZhitnaya. 2–3 – clarst5, Kumeko, brgfx, Black_Rhino. 4–5 – emper71, kemper31, ST-art. 6–7 – Urban Furniture, Fotografas Edgaras. 8–9 – Goinyk Production, andreiuc88. 10–11 – Ground Picture, DrimaFilm. 12–13 – Alik Mulikov, Jacquie Klose. 14–15 – CTatiana, John Glade.